SLAMMING OPEN THE DOOR

Slamming Open the Door

Kathleen Sheeder Bonanno

ALICE JAMES BOOKS | FARMINGTON, MAINE

13 12 11 10 9 8 7 6 5 4

Alice James Books are published by Alice James Poetry Cooperative, Inc.,
an affiliate of the University of Maine at Farmington.

ALICE JAMES BOOKS
238 MAIN STREET
FARMINGTON, ME 04938

www.alicejamesbooks.org

Library of Congress Cataloging-in-Publication Data

Bonanno, Kathleen Sheeder, 1955 –
  Slamming open the door / Kathleen Sheeder Bonanno.
    p. cm.
  ISBN-13: 978-1-882295-74-6
  ISBN-10: 1-882295-74-9
  I. Title.
  PS3602.O6562S58 2009
  811'.6—dc22   2009001735

Alice James Books gratefully acknowledges support from the Univer-
sity of Maine at Farmington and the National Endowment for the Arts.

Photograph of Leidy courtesy of the author
Cover image: © Veer Incorporated

ACKNOWLEDGEMENTS

Thanks to the editors of *The Women's Review of Books* where "Tea Time" and "Ice Skating" originally appeared.

Excerpt from the article "Woman Strangled in West Reading" reprinted with permission of *The Reading Eagle*.

My heartfelt thanks to David Bonanno, Luis Bonanno, Suzanne Sheeder, Caitlin Sheeder-Borrelli, Joseph Borrelli, Norine and Rich Bonanno, Rebecca Bonanno, Rick Topper, Brian Smith, Susan Boland, Emily Boland, Kate Brenton, Victoria Murphy, Kent Matthies, Bernadette Lloyd Sobolow, Teresa Leo, Daniel Tobin, Joan Houlihan, C. K. Williams, Peter Waldor, Anne Marie Macari, Gerald Stern and Ellen Doré Watson for their encouragement and wise counsel during the creation of this book.

And finally, my gratitude to the best editorial staff any poet could wish for—April Ossmann, Carey Salerno, Lacy Simons and Shelli-Jo Pelletier.

My love to our family, friends, and the members of the Unitarian Society of Germantown, who stood by us during our hardest time.

LEIDY SHEEDER BONANNO

CONTENTS

DEATH BARGED IN

In his Russian greatcoat,
slamming open the door
with an unpardonable bang,
and he has been here ever since.

He changes everything,
rearranges the furniture,
his hand hovers
by the phone;
he will answer now, he says;
he will be the answer.

Tonight he sits down to dinner
at the head of the table
as we eat, mute;
later, he climbs into bed
between us.

Even as I sit here,
he stands behind me
clamping two
colossal hands on my shoulders
and bends down
and whispers to my neck:
From now on,
you write about me.

HOW TO FIND OUT

◆

After you call her
again and again
on her home phone,
and your intention,
like a mouse in a snake's belly,
swells the wire
as it runs from one pole
to another
and still she doesn't answer—

after you call her
on her cell phone
and summon a satellite network
to assist,
to bounce your voice
from your house
to a floating point in space,
to her house,
and still she doesn't answer—

after you leave many messages,
and your husband leaves messages,
and your sister leaves messages,
and anxiety flits over and around you—

ignore it. She is an adult now.
Wait a day.

◆

First leave a final message:
We are going to drive

up there right now, young lady,
if you don't call us back in fifteen minutes.

And then start driving
in a hard rain,
you and Dave,
and when you get to Skippack
your cell phone will ring
and someone will say
she was just spotted
working her nursing shift
on the hospital floor.

Laugh and turn the car around then—
a ton of relief
barreling back down Route 73.

When you get home,
call the hospital,
just to make sure.

◆

Her supervisor will say
No, no, she's not here;
she hasn't shown up for work
in two days.

This is the time
for your throat to thicken,
for your fingers to get rubbery,
for you to call the police

and say, *Please please*
go to her apartment and
if it's locked, please
knock down the door.

♦

Now you and your husband
and sister and her husband
must jump into his car
and drive so fast you might crash;

hold your husband's hand hard
but do not look at him,
do not look him in the eyes
until one of you says,

Jesus, I have to go to the bathroom,
and all four of you run
into a diner somewhere
and as the patrons look up,
charge into the restroom
and pee hard,

so you don't wet your clothes later,
and take a moment
to dry heave a little into the toilet,
but not too much, there's no time.

♦

Pull up onto her street.
Jump out of the moving car
as your brother-in-law parks it.

Run past police cars,
ambulance,
all the silent people
sitting on curbs,
gathered on porches,
their arms folded

waiting for you,
the parents,
to arrive.

The chief of police,
poised behind the yellow tape,
will spread his long arms to you,
his palms outward.
This is it:
your very own
annunciation.

Try to be thoughtful,
don't make the poor man say it;
see how human he is,
he has children of his own,
it is your job to ask:
Is she dead?

And he will nod and say *yes.*
And now he can never not nod.
And now he can never say no.
And now he can never not say
yes.

WOMAN STRANGLED
IN WEST READING
Recent nursing grad Leidy Bonanno
knew her killer, investigators believe
by Keith Mayer, *Reading Eagle*

Leidy S. Bonanno, 21,
was found dead
late Tuesday
inside her first floor apartment. . . .
The killer used
Bonanno's telephone cord
to choke her
then left her body on her bed.
[He] covered her face
with a bed pillow,
and locked the apartment
doors [before he] left,
police said.

MEETING YOU, AGE FOUR

You have waved goodbye already,
we have waved already,
you have waved again until
there's nothing left
for us to do with dignity but go.

We back out of the lot
in one large economic swoop,
like a giant hand
has yanked us from behind.

You lift a sober little chin,
your face full upon us
as we pull away.

The funny sound
we need to fix begins
from under the inscrutable hood
of the old Maverick.
A tiny, tinny ball
riding a roulette wheel,
waiting to pick a number.

I do not need to look at David.
He does not need to look at me.
We drive straight home.
We look ahead.
The little ball whirrs:
We want you, we want you, we want you.

AUTOPSY REPORT

Hair: dark like the woods
Eyes: tender
Nose: Mayan
Teeth: white, wide
Mouth: Oh, God,
who drives the poem,
do not make me think of her mouth,
how it laughed.

Heart: full
Other Internal Organs:
perfect, each
Cause of Death:
ligature strangulation
Last Recorded
Image on Retina:
someone who wanted her
not
to tell.

NIGHTTIME PRAYER

Did she suffer, did she suffer,
Hail Mary full of grace,
did she suffer?

Our Father,
Who art in heaven,
how much,
how much,
Hallowed be Thy name,

Thy kingdom come,
Thy will be done,
was it long was it long was it long,
was it one,
was it two was it three,
was it ten was it this,
when she suffered

On earth as it is in
how she saw,
what she saw,
what she saw,
what last,

Did she suffer,
did she
didshe
What.
Last.

U.S.S. JUNEAU

Seaman Luis Bonanno, asleep in his berth,
dreaming of the Straits of Malaca,
wakes to a sailor saying,
The First Lieutenant wants to see you.
The Lieutenant says, *The Chaplain wants to see you.*
The Chaplain says, *Sit down.*

When Luis Bonanno stands up
and hurls the chaplain's computer at him,
the Master of Arms and three enlisted men
rush in. They hold his elbows, steer him—
an unwilling date—back to his berth,
while he cries, and his nose drips,
and he takes random punches
where he can.

His mates shove his clothes
into his duffle bag, money into his overalls,
tell him, *Here, buy her flowers
from the deckbums of the Juneau.*

HEARSAY

Hearsay is inadmissible.
Hearsay is what she told me
on the phone the night
before she died.
Hearsay is how I know he did it.

She said she slept with him.
She said she broke up with him.

She said he stole
her social security number
to get a credit card
to buy motorcycle parts,

that he was a phlebotomist
and could call up her data
on the hospital computer.

She said she called his supervisor
to report him for identity theft.

She said she thought
he made a copy of her key,

that she would call
her landlord
to have her locks changed.

She said *Okay, Mom, okay,*
I won't sleep here tonight;
I promise.

STICKS AND STONES

To you, who killed my daughter—
Run. Run. Hide.
Tell your mother
to thread the needle
made of bone.
It is *her* time now
to sew the shroud.

The men are coming
with sticks and stones
and whetted spears
to do what needs doing.

WHAT PEOPLE GIVE YOU

Long-faced irises. Mums.
Pink roses and white roses
and giant sunflowers,
and hundreds of daisies.

Fruit baskets with muscular pears,
and water crackers and tiny jams
and the steady march of casseroles.
And money,
people give money these days.

Cards, of course:
the Madonna, wise
and sad just for you,
Chinese cherry blossoms,
sunsets and moonscapes,
and dragonflies for transcendence.

People stand by your sink
and offer up their pain:
Did you know I lost a baby once,
or *My eldest son was killed,*
or *My mother died two months ago.*

People are good.
They file into your cartoon house
until it bows at the seams;
they give you every
blessed
thing,
everything,
except your daughter back.

NURSING SCHOOL GRADUATION PARTY

Six Weeks Before

We laugh and pile our plates high
with chicken and sirloin tips.
For party favors—pots of pansies
and little chocolate ladybugs
from Germany.

At every setting a photo
of Leidy in her nursing cap.

Deborah tells about the time
Barbara Walters stepped on her foot
and didn't say excuse me,
or maybe Deborah
stepped on Barbara's foot.

Kirsten's son Austin
wears a grown-up tie
and a black spider
painted on his cheek.

Uncle Jeff from New Jersey
starts to pick a little on the banjo,
and the good men from church
clap and pull their chairs close to him.

We sing a song to Leidy
that I wrote to the tune of
"She'll Be Coming 'Round the Mountain"
and I lead the chorus,
waving a broomstick
painted like a giant thermometer.

When Dave clears his throat,
and raises his glass to toast her,
we raise our glasses, too—
and Johnny Early, a nice young man
from Reading Hospital,
smiles and raises his glass.

THE HAIR

Bernadette in blue jeans,
and Suzanne in her swishy skirt and boots,
in another time
would have worn veils
and wailed at the wall for her,
or washed her gently
and prayed for her Victorian soul,
or put pennies on her eyes
for the ferryman.

Today they work with what they've got—
one healthy hank of hair,
chopped off the back of her head
by the funeral director.

They shampoo it three times
until it smells like honeysuckle,
brush it and tie it and lay
the curling bundles
on the dining room table.

They put one in an abalone box,
one in an amber box,
one in a wooden box,
and one in a locket for me
to fasten around my neck.

WHAT NOT TO SAY

Don't say that you choked
on a chicken bone once,
and then make the sound,
kuh, kuh, and say
you bet that's how she felt.

Don't ask in horror
why we cremated her.

And when I stand
in the receiving line
like Jackie Kennedy
without the pillbox hat,
if Jackie were fat
and had taken
enough Klonopin
to still an ox,

and you whisper,
*I think of you
every day,*
don't finish with
*because I've been going
to Weight Watchers
on Tuesdays and wonder
if you want to go too.*

HOMICIDE DETECTIVE

In the morning
we rush up to him
where he stands
in Leidy's misbegotten little yard
looking at the dirt.
I think, *Is this*
what gathering clues looks like?

But his is the voice of water.
Only he knows the right words to say,
and he says them:
I promise we will get this guy.

When I show him a photo
he says, *She's beautiful;*
almost how she looked
when we found her.

And now I know who to believe.
What does the coroner, who says
she had maggots in her mouth,
know about the truth?

RED SATURN

My car is a soundproof capsule
moving through space,
and sometimes I wail in it.
White Greek mask,
open-mouthed grimace
hanging above the wheel.

You may have seen
my big, fat tragic face
zooming by,
or at a stoplight, once.

Someone should stop me.
I cry, therefore I am
unable to see,
therefore,
I turn on the windshield wipers.

When I pull up beside you,
walking your dog,
I pity you, I do.

My ghastly smile,
my comedy mask,
popping up
from the driver's side window,
my teeth a little yellow,
Excuse me, excuse me,
can you tell me
where to turn?

REWARD

The reporters with their caravans
and collapsible equipment
rush in and out
and in between,
adopt an earnest air
and point the microphone
in your direction.

Oh yes, you have something to say.
There is a reward
of ten thousand dollars
for information
leading to the arrest
of our daughter's killer.

And if they want
to photograph you
clutching her nursing school portrait,
or hugging your son,
or standing by the makeshift altar
gazing soberly into the camera,
so what? So you let them.

WILD WEST

When the townsfolk gather
and shake their heads,
and cast their eyes downward,

thankful that their own daughters
are home right now,
humming a little,
pulling pies from the oven,

and the town drunk,
in memory of that poor lil' girl,
takes another suck
off the bottle,

and Good Ole' Doc wonders aloud
if evil is born into us,
or we go out to meet it,

and Old Mrs. Johnson
with the quivering feather
on her bonnet whispers,
*That girl always was too boy crazy
for her own good—*

right about then,
Sheriff Rodriquez
and two of his deputies
will stand up,
horses neighing and pawing the dirt
where they're tethered,
and say, *Let's go.*

And as they gallop away,
they'll look back
and spot you in the distance,
trying to catch up,
horse huffing, wet apron flapping,
pupils like bullets.

KIDNEY STONE

My daughter was murdered
and God, like a hack,
cannot let it be for awhile,
in its Shakespearean elegance
to shimmer and twang
like a dagger thrust into wood,

so now, I have a kidney stone, too,
a big one, and they are whisking me
into a green operating room
at Holy Redeemer Hospital,
where a sinewy little Jesus sags
on a crucifix on the wall.

But first, afraid, on the litter,
I say to my sister,
What if I don't wake up
from the anesthesia?
and she presses my hand
and says, *No, no,*
don't even think that way—
you are not that lucky.

WILLIAM

Your young friend, William,
who you have not heard from
because he just had a baby, a son,
and so he is glorious
and drunk in the light
of human nature,

will one day decide
to walk all the way
from his place in the universe

to yours.
And there he will be,
on the doorstep
with his dachshund
under one arm,
and a thawing cake in a box
under the other.

And when you
open the storm door
to let him in,
he will step onto the mat,
and bow his head a little,
and cry like a man.

ICE SKATING

Our daughter is gone now,
forever, a tragedy,
so we skate way far over in the distance,
remotely visible,
two pitiable lurchers
where the surface is wafery thin
and the light is bad,
where no one would choose to skate
had God not pointed an icy,
peremptory finger
and said, *There.*

But you, you
and your family,
with your bulky knitted sweaters
and whimsical peaked caps,
you are right in the center
where the ice looks safe,
and your daughter laughs hard,
two bright pink spots
high on her cheeks,
as she glides backward,
exhaling her breathy love for you.

CONFESSIONS

Don't pity me:
I was too lazy to walk
up the stairs
to tuck her in at night.

When I brushed her hair
I pulled hard
on purpose.

And always—
the sharp,
plaintive edge
on the rim
of the spoon
of my giving.

ANT

An ant rears its front legs,
its rosary-bead parts
startling and black,
but I do not see it.

You name it.
I cannot see
what she can
not see.

THE UNITARIAN SOCIETY OF GERMANTOWN

The church is a big wooden boat,
Dave and I in a corner,
as the rain drops patter
then slash
through the dark outside.

Hold on tight,
says the kindly moon face
of the minister.

But we can smell our own sweat.
We roll our eyes and moan
and grapple for position.

One by one, the others
press their bodies against us,
until finally,
we tire and lean in
to their patient animal breath,
to wait it out together.

PRE-TRIAL HEARING
He Pleads Not Guilty

Poor man,
you are clutching
at each slender wrong
ever done to you,
by anyone,
each tiny outrage
a pale reedy stalk of grass
jutting from the bank.

But the truth tugs hard
at your feet, doesn't it?
And it threatens to pull you down
into the vast lake
of your own undoing.
Let go, my friend.

Let go, and take the long tour under.
See, on the bottom,
a woman, young,
her brown hair
undulating in the water,
her eyes open,

but wait,
see the telephone cord wrapped
around her neck
three times,
and tied into a knot?
Look how the little ends
of the cord
wave to you.

SWOOPING

My sister says
maybe Johnny Early will try to run
from the courtroom
and Detective Joseph Murano
(who should have his own TV show),
will pull out his gun
and shoot him, and then
swoop her into his arms.

There will be no swooping,
I say, unamused,
think of your husband.
But I am thinking of mine,

who says that I can
have anything, anything,
I want that might please me.
And I say, *Okay, I want*
to have an affair,
or I want a teacup Chihuahua.

And my husband says,
Yes, alright,
maybe the affair,
because dogs are a lot of work.

BIRTHDAY POEM

It is our dead daughter's birthday.
Her name was Leidy, pronounced Lady.
We adopted her from Chile.
Her nickname when she was little
was Ladybug.

I sit in a dining room chair
and cry hard,
while my neck bends
in increments
until my forehead touches the table.

People are waiting for us
at her favorite restaurant
and my husband says finally,
Kathy, it's time to go,
as he reaches his hand into his pocket
for his car keys
and pulls it out again,
a live ladybug
resting there.

BLUE RECLINERS

We will be here
in our matching blue recliners
as night falls
and the TV flickers.

The front door
will open slowly,
and she will peek
her head in first,
smiling on tiptoe,
and say *Shhhhhhh*
like a vaudevillian thief.

A mistake! we'll shout and laugh,
as we struggle
from our chairs.
Can you believe it?
as our little dog twirls.

COMMUNION

When your minister
proposes *forgiveness*—
because, after all, he must—
he lifts the word
like a wafer,
into air.

You counter
by hoisting the cup of wine.
Here's to hate, you say,
slugging it back,
eyeing the dregs.

VENIRE

No, I whisper, *not number 47,*
who just admitted
he pled guilty, once,
to stalking his ex-girlfriend
on the telephone.

But the D.A. thinks maybe he's a keeper,
squints his eyes,
cranes his neck for a better look,
thinks maybe we could do worse.

In the end,
the judge swears in sixteen of them,
with names like Jay
and Warren and Kelly Ann.
Oh, June, with your big glasses
you could be me,
Catherine, your long hair
like Leidy's.

All of us uncertain
in the heavy air,
our stars crossing
above us.

LIFE IN PRISON

If you are convicted,
if you are sentenced
to life in prison without parole,

you, who murdered my daughter,
you, with four children of your own,
I will say

Oh, I wish I were lucky
like you
to see my child again
on some unnamed day,

through a pane of glass,
to nearly touch
my larger hand to hers.

Oh, what I would give
to see her
through a hundred panes of glass,
a thousand of them,
each a generous window to a window
to her,

The familiar curve of her neck,
her wide smile,
her thick hair,
raising her hand to wave,
me waving too,
Look, I'm here,
I'm here.

TEA TIME

Losing your daughter,
losing your daughter to murder,
requires adjustment.

Like, say,
you are sipping tea
and someone
reaches over and
fantastically yanks
your heart from your chest

and it drops, pumping,
onto the table
and there it is,
there is the matter,
your whole heart,
that brilliant engine,

that tuber,
vulgar, purple,
red

and you simply don't die,
you see;
you blanch,
and your brain beats on
and then, and then,

invariably,
you reach down
to straighten a spoon.

THE PROSECUTOR

Boom goes his voice;
he hitches up his giant pants.
His eyebrows are the intersection
of the Tigris and Euphrates.

Hear me, groans
the sacred text of evidence,
a thousand pages,
Hear me.

Scritch, scritch
go the bony feet
of the defense attorneys
as they run for cover.

And now he draws the sword—
Whissssh through the neck
of Johnny Early.
O, says Johnny Early's mouth
as his head falls
down,
up, the prosecutor flings it
by the hair,
up, it tumbles

through the air,
through the ceiling,
through the sky
past the weary
eye of God.

And we
would throw ourselves
weeping into his arms,
O Beloved Unequivocator,
but he cannot allow this,
already striding away.

DEFENSE ATTORNEY

You lean into him,
like a kind mother
in sensible trousers,
and he looks up at you
with his full face,
his animal hands quiet
in the metal cuffs
in his lap.

You murmur and smile
and pin your eyes to his,
be brave, be brave,
until he smiles back.

And where were *you,*
I wonder,
in the early hours
of July 7th
before you knew him,
your man-client,
before you had even dreamt him.

Were you asleep,
in the dark?
Were you resting?
Were you comfortable,

when he tore the telephone cord
from the wall,
your busy, busy, boy,
and wrapped it
around her neck
and began to pull?

THE VERDICT IS IN

They deliberate for four hours
while we sit downstairs in the cafeteria
where none of us can swallow food
until the bailiff says it's time.

And then we run, *run*
back to the courtroom.
Four hours, is that a short time?
A long time? A good sign?
A bad sign?

My father, who cannot see,
my mother with her cane,
Murfie from New York,
Rudi Springer from church,
the nurses, the officers,
lawyers I have never seen before,
everybody, everybody

and then a middle-aged
woman, unrelated
to our side or his,
with starchy hair
and a pointed curiosity,

decides to get a good seat
in the front row next to me.
I say, *You have to move:*
this row is for my family.

She does not move.
As if her legal rights matter
here, of all places,
so I say what I mean:
Don't fuck with me now.
And she moves.

And Holly, that reporter I like,
gives her a glare for good measure,
turns to me,
and smiles sweetly. . . .

then Suzanne starts
to squeeze my left hand
and David starts to squeeze
my right.

CHURCH OF JUSTICE

Guilty, say the jurors.
We gasp and sigh
and hug and weep
just like on TV.

We walk down the aisle
and a woman waits
in the hallway for me.
She says my name.

I have studied her,
Johnny Early's mother,
and despise her,
and the son she carried,
and the Bible she carries.

She says,
I am so sorry.
Suddenly she is tiny;
she has a tooth missing
from the bottom row.

She holds out her arms
and what can I do,
what,
but hug her back,
my truest other sister.
She says,
I am so sorry.

TO JOHN EARLY'S SON

Did you think we were enemies?
I am on a road, you
are on a parallel road
with just a sliver of wind
between us—
I can almost feel your shoulder.

People stare at my back.
People stare at your back.
We each walk fast
looking for goodness,
looking for someone
else's life.

LADYBUGS

We see them everywhere now.
Last month, a tiny baby one
more orange than red,
purposeful, crawling
on the wall
above my side of the bed.

Inside a domed reception hall
at a fund-raising supper,
in the middle
of our round table
sits a perfect dead one.

We eat our soup
until one of us spots it,
our spoons slowing.

My niece wraps it in a pink tissue,
as if it were a sequin dropped
from the sleeve of God,
and takes it home.

After the trial, a blizzard
of ladybugs on the courthouse steps,
more this week
than Berks County has seen in years.
At first we crunch them underfoot
until, horrified, we look down
and know what we do.

Hundreds of them,
shining orange and black,
the dead and the living together—
the living
on the backs of the dead.

ANOTHER MOTHER

Parents of Murdered Children Conference

We have everything in common.
She is Texan and her husband is a trucker.
She wears white spangly boots
to cocktail hour,
and sells fibre optic lapel pins
of Jesus on a blinking cross.

If we were Irish women
on the road at dusk,
I would link arms with her.
If we were in a trench,
I would burst forward to save her,
my heart an exploding corsage.

Today she confesses
she keeps her son's room
just as it was four years ago —
the bed, his socks,
the complicated terrain
of his dresser,
even the trash in his trash can
the same.

I think of the crumbs,
and apple cores,
the pea-sized wads of gum wrappers,
the hieroglyph of dried mucus
on the Kleenex.
Of course, I say to myself.

HOLY MARY TRAMPOLINE GIRL

You are six,
a blue scarf laid over your head,
soberly pinned under your chin,
and a red lipsticky mouth,
like some floozy mother of Jesus.

You scramble up onto my giant bed
and start bouncing, just a little
at first, knee bends really,
and look side-wise to see if I'll yell—
and then bigger and bigger
kangaroo boy jumps,

my giant pleated skirt
pulled up under your armpits,
puffing out like a jellyfish as you jump,
bangs flying,
veil flapping;
as you bounce
and hitch your elbows into the air
to meet the moment
more than halfway.

GRADUATION PARTY PHOTOGRAPH

Leidy, dark and lovely
sits on my ample lap
and presses her cheek hard
against my cheek.

I wear an unfortunate floral dress
and am flushed pink
with pride in her.

My hand and her hand
hold tight, together on her knee,

Each of us sure
we have been through the worst of it:
the biting metal exchanges
about her curfew,
her boyfriend,
her contact lenses,
any old thing.

Women now,
we smile our love
for the rest of time
straight back
into God's eye.

POEM ABOUT LIGHT

You can try to strangle light:
use your hands and think
you've found the throat of it,
but you haven't.
You could use a rope or a garrote
or a telephone cord,
but the light, amorphous, implacable,
will make a fool of you in the end.

You could make it your mission
to shut it out forever,
to crouch in the dark,
the blinds pulled tight—

still, in the morning,
a gleaming little ray will betray you, poking
its optimistic finger
through a corner of the blind,
and then more light,
clever, nervy, impossible,
spilling out from the crevices
warming the shade.

This is the stubborn sun,
choosing to rise,
like it did yesterday,
like it will tomorrow.
You have nothing to do with it.
The sun makes its own history;
light has its way.

ALICE JAMES BOOKS has been publishing exclusively poetry since 1973. One of the few presses in the country that is run collectively, the cooperative selects manuscripts for publication through both regional and national annual competitions. New regional authors become active members of the cooperative, participating in the editorial decisions of the press. The press, which historically has placed an emphasis on publishing women poets, was named for Alice James, sister of William and Henry, whose fine journal and gift for writing went unrecognized within her lifetime.

Typeset and Designed by Christopher Kuntze

Printed by Thomson-Shore
on 30% postconsumer recycled paper
processed chlorine-free